THE BARBECUE
COOKBOOK

Photography by Peter Barry
Recipes styled by Jacqueline Bellefontaine
Designed by Richard Hawke and Claire Leighton
Edited by Jillian Stewart and Kate Cranshaw

3559
© 1994 Coombe Books
This edition published in 1994 by Coombe Books
for Parragon Book Service Ltd., Unit 13-17,
Avonbridge Trading Estate, Atlantic Road,
Avonbridge, Bath
All rights reserved.
Printed in Hong Kong
ISBN 1-85813-467-6

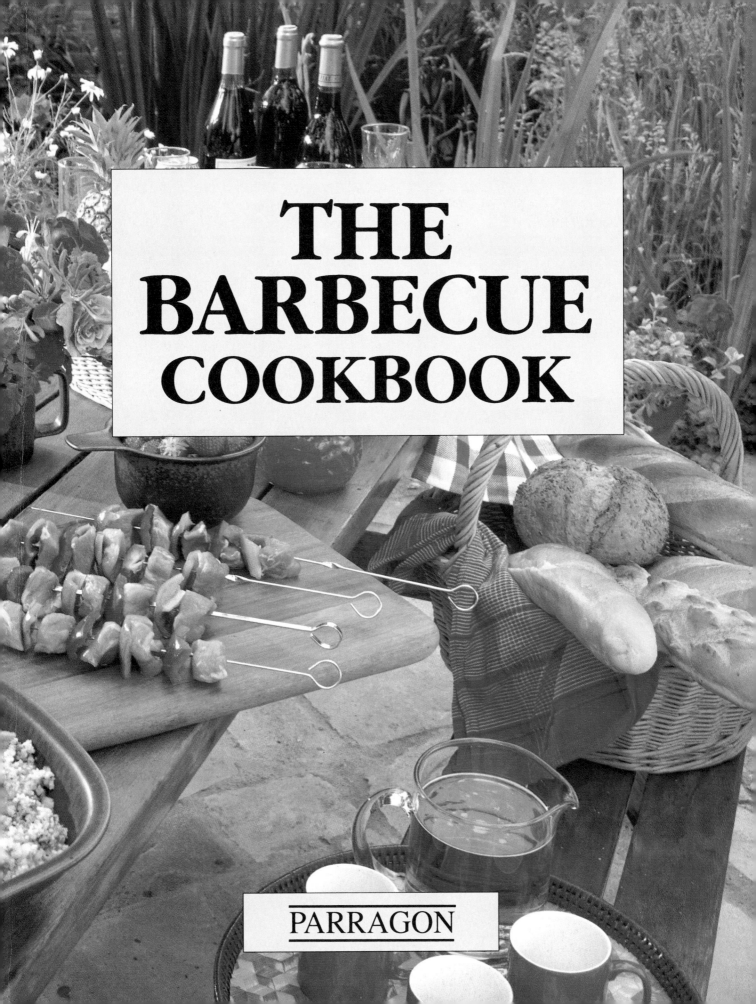

THE BARBECUE COOKBOOK

PARRAGON

Contents

Introduction

Everyone enjoys a barbecue, whether as a alternative family Sunday lunch or a large informal party. The secret of success is planning and organisation, and although we cannot control the weather, we can ensure that everything runs as smoothly as possible.

The first thing to consider is the barbecue. There are several types of barbecue available, ranging from the small disposable picnic type – ideal for a countryside or beach barbecue for two or three people, to the semi-portable grill on wheels, or the 'no sweat no mess' electric and gas grills. For serious barbecuing, whatever the type, some basic features are a must – a windshield; a fire bowl with ventilation holes, to allow the air to circulate freely; and an adjustable grill rack to help regulate the cooking.

The best type of fuel to use is compressed charcoal briquettes, as these burn for twice as long and with a more uniform heat than lumpwood charcoal. To start the coals, firelighter fuel or blocks are the quickest method, but for safety reasons these should never be added to hot coals. A barbecue is only ready to cook on after the flames have died down and the coals are covered with a layer of ash. This acts as insulation and should be flicked off before cooking. Using the appropriate equipment is also essential for successful results. For the fire, a pair of bellows or a fan helps increase the heat; a clean water-filled plant sprayer is useful to douse any flare up of flames; for cooking whole fish, hamburgers, steaks and chops, hinged wire racks make turning quick and simple; and long-handled utensils such as tongs, a fork and a natural bristle brush prevent burnt fingers.

Cooking times for barbecued food are never very exact as different types of barbecues create varying degrees of heat. To tell roughly how hot your barbecue is, hold your hand above the coals at the height of the grill rack, if you can keep your hand there whilst saying 'Mississippi' once, the barbecue is producing high heat. If you can say it twice before having to remove your hand, the heat is medium, three times and the heat is low. To ensure that the meat is cooked through before the outside becomes charred, the meat should be no more than 4 cm/1½ inches thick and should be at room temperature before grilling. To sear the meat and seal in all its juices, the oiled grill rack should be lowered to the position nearest the coals, or the heat increased briefly by using a pair of bellows. Once the meat is seared on both sides, the grill should be raised to allow the meat to cook more slowly.

Aside from barbecued foods, it is usual to serve a good selection of salads as their refreshing flavours are the perfect way of counteracting the rich, spiciness of the meat. The most important point to remember is that barbecues are supposed to be good fun, so relax and enjoy yourself. After all, a barbecue is one of the few times the hosts can actually involve their guests in cooking the food!

GRILLED SARDINES WITH LEMON AND OREGANO

These sardines could be served as a starter or a main course. Cook the fish in an oiled wire rack if you have one.

SERVES 4-6

8-12 sprigs fresh oregano
8-12 fresh sardines, gutted, scaled, washed and dried
90ml/3 fl oz olive oil
Juice and rind of 2 lemons
Salt and pepper
1 tbsp dried oregano

1. Place one sprig of oregano inside each fish. Mix the oil, lemon juice and rind, salt and pepper together.

2. Make two slits on each side of the fish.

3. Brush the fish with the lemon mixture and grill over hot coals for 3-4 minutes per side, basting frequently.

4. When the fish are nearly done, sprinkle the dried oregano on the coals. The smoke will give the fish extra flavour. Serve immediately.

TIME: Preparation takes about 10 minutes, and cooking takes 6-8 minutes.

VARIATION: Use othe larger whole fish such as herrings, pilchards, or mackerel and increase cooking time.

MARSALA FISH

Fish cooks very well on a barbecue and is best cooked quite quickly using a wire fish rack, as it makes turning so much easier.

SERVES 4

4 medium sized mackerel, trout or similar
    fish, cleaned and gutted
Fresh coriander leaves
Juice of 1 lemon
2 tsps turmeric
2 green chillies, finely chopped
1 small piece ginger, grated
1 clove garlic, crushed
Pinch ground cinnamon
Pinch ground cloves
60ml/4 tbsps oil
Salt and pepper

Sauce
½ cucumber, finely diced
140ml/¼ pint thick natural yogurt
1 spring onion, finely chopped
Salt and pepper

1. Cut three slits on each side of the fish.

2. Place whole sprigs of coriander inside the fish.

3. Combine the lemon juice, spices, oil, garlic and chillies and spread over the fish and inside the cuts.

4. Brush the grill rack or a wire fish rack lightly with oil. Cook the fish for 10-15 minutes, over hot coals, turning often and basting with any remaining mixture.

5. Combine the sauce ingredients and serve with the fish.

TIME: Preparation takes 15 minutes and cooking takes 10-15 minutes.

VARIATION: Use fish steaks instead and marinate in the flavouring ingredients for 2-3 hours. Alter cooking time accordingly.

ORANGE GRILLED DUCK WITH SESAME AND SPICE

If you like rare steak cook the duck breast to the same degree – it tastes really delicious. Serve with a mixed leaf salad.

SERVES 4

4 boned duck breasts
60ml/4 tbsps sesame seeds

Marinade
60ml/4 tbsps soy sauce
120ml/4 fl oz dry white wine
3 tbsps oil
Pinch ground nutmeg
Pinch ground ginger
Pinch ground mustard
Salt and pepper

Sauce
Reserved marinade
175ml/6 fl oz orange juice
1 shallot, finely chopped
2 tsps cornflour

Garnish
1 orange, peel and pith removed, flesh
    thinly sliced
Brown sugar

1. Score the fat side of each duck breast with a sharp knife.

2. Mix the marinade ingredients together and pour over the duck in a shallow dish. Cover and refrigerate for 2 hours, turning the duck frequently.

3. Place the duck breasts fat side down on a lightly oiled grill over hot coals. Cook for 4-7 minutes for rare duck, or 10-12 minutes for more cooked meat. Baste frequently. If the duck appears to be cooking too quickly, turn and baste more often.

4. Combine the sauce ingredients and add any remaining marinade. Cook for 1-2 minutes over a moderate heat until boiling.

5. Just before the duck is finished cooking, brush the fat side lightly with the sauce and sprinkle on the sesame seeds.

6. Turn fat side down onto the grill for 1 minute. Serve the remaining sauce with the duck.

7. To prepare the garnish, five minutes before the duck is cooked, sprinkle the orange slices with some brown sugar and grill on both sides to glaze. Serve with the duck.

TIME: Preparation takes 15 minutes plus 2 hours marinating time. Cooking takes between 8 and 24 minutes, depending on taste.

PREPARATION: Allow the duck to come to room temperature before cooking.

BUTTERFLIED LAMB

A butterflied leg of lamb, (one that has been boned and flattened out) is ideal for a Sunday lunch barbecue instead of traditional roast lamb – and it's much quicker to cook too.

SERVES 6-8

1.8kg/4lb leg of lamb
75ml/5 tbsps oil
Juice and rind of 1 lemon
Small bunch mint, roughly chopped
Salt and coarsely ground black pepper
1 clove garlic, crushed

1. To butterfly the lamb, turn the joint upside down and locate the irregular shaped pelvic bone at the top end of the leg, which runs at an angle to the main leg bone. Using a small sharp knife, scrape all around the bone to remove it, severing the tendons at the ball and socket joint.

2. Next, at the other end of the leg, cut all the tendons at the end of the shank bone. Scrape the meat away from the bone up to the knee joint, cut the tendons, and remove the bone.

3. Now cut down the centre of the leg along the line of the remaining bone. Cut out the bone and remove excess fat. Flatten thick places by making shallow cuts halfway through the thickest parts and pressing open.

4. Thread two or three long skewers through the meat – this will make the meat easier to handle and turn when cooking.

5. Place in a plastic bag or shallow dish. Mix the other ingredients together and pour over the lamb, rubbing it in well.

6. Cover the dish or seal the bag and leave overnight in the refrigerator. Turn the lamb frequently.

7. Remove from the dish or the bag and reserve the marinade.

8. Grill at least 15cm/6 inches away from the coals on the skin side first. Grill, basting frequently, for 15-20 minutes per side for pink lamb and 30 minutes per side for well done lamb.

9. Remove the skewers and cut the slices across the grain to serve.

TIME: Preparation takes about 30 minutes plus overnight marinating. Cooking takes 40 minutes to 1 hour.

PREPARATION: Allow the lamb to come to room temperature before cooking.

COOK'S TIP: A butcher will butterfly the lamb for you.

Niçoise Chicken

*This chicken is cooked in the style of Nice in southern France – with tomatoes,
garlic, capers, olives and lemon.*

SERVES 4

4 boned chicken breasts, unskinned
60ml/4 tbsps oil
2 tbsps lemon juice

Tapenade Filling
460g/1lb large black olives, pitted
2 tbsps capers
1 clove garlic, roughly chopped
4 canned anchovy fillets
2 tbsps olive oil

Raw Tomato Sauce
460g/1lb ripe tomatoes, skinned, seeded
   and chopped
1 shallot, very finely chopped
2 tbsps chopped parsely
2 tbsps chopped basil
2 tbsps white wine vinegar
2 tbsps olive oil
1 tbsp sugar
Salt and pepper
1 tbsp tomato purée (optional)

1. Cut a pocket in the thickest side of the chicken breasts.

2. To prepare the filling, purée half the olives, half the capers and the remaining ingredients for the tapenade together in a blender or food processor.

3. Add the remaining olives and capers and process a few times to chop them roughly.

4. Fill the chicken breasts with the tapenade and chill to help the filling to firm.

5. Baste the skin side with oil and lemon juice mixed mixed together and cook skin side down, for 10 minutes over medium hot coals.

6. Turn over, baste again and grill for another 10 minutes on the other side.

7. Meanwhile, combine the raw sauce ingredients and mix very well. Serve with the chicken.

TIME: Preparation takes 30 minutes and cooking takes 20 minutes.

PREPARATION: To skin the tomatoes easily, just pierce the skins and plunge
into boiling water for 30 seconds. Drain, refresh in cold water.

HERB AND ONION GRILLED LAMB CHOPS

These chops are quick to prepare. The marinade gives them a lovely flavour and keeps the meat moist during cooking.

SERVES 4

4 leg chops, cut 2cm/¾-inch thick

Marinade
1 large onion, finely chopped
1 tbsp parsley, finely chopped
1 tbsp fresh thyme or mint leaves, roughly chopped
2 fresh bay leaves, bruised
1 clove garlic, crushed
3 tbsps oil
Juice of ½ lemon
Salt and pepper

1. Combine all the marinade ingredients and pour over the chops in a dish.

2. Cover and marinate for 2 hours in the refrigerator.

3. Place the chops on a rack over hot coals and cook for about 15 minutes, turning often and basting frequently with the remaining marinade.

TIME: Preparation takes 10 minutes plus 2 hours marinating. Cooking takes about 15 minutes.

COOK'S TIP: Allow the meat to come to room temperature before cooking.

19

19

STUFFED HAMBURGERS

Choose two of the variations to flavour the basic meat mix, and impress your friends with these gourmet burgers.

SERVES 4-8

900g/2lbs minced beef
1 onion, finely chopped
60ml/4 tbsps Worcesterhsire sauce
Salt and pepper
8 hamburger buns

GUACAMOLE BURGERS

Filling

120g/4oz Tilsit cheese, cubed
1 mild chilli, thinly sliced and seeds
   removed

Topping

1 avocado, peeled and mashed
1 small clove garlic, crushed
2 tsps lemon or lime juice
1 tomato, skinned, seeded and finely
   chopped
Salt and pepper

BLUE CHEESE BURGERS

Filling

120g/4oz blue cheese, crumbled
30g/1oz chopped walnuts

Topping

1 tbsp brown sauce
75ml/5 tbsps mayonnaise
90ml/6 tbsps soured cream or yogurt
Salt and pepper

GRUYÈRE AND MUSHROOM BURGERS

Filling

60g/2oz mushrooms, roughly chopped

120g/4oz Gruyère or Swiss cheese, cubed

Topping

460g/1lb tomatoes
1 clove garlic, finely chopped
2 tbsps chopped tarragon
1 tbsp tarragon vinegar
Pinch salt
2 tbsps oil
Salt and pepper

1. Thoroughly mix together the beef, onion, Worcestershire sauce and salt and pepper.

2. Divide the meat mixture into burger-sized portions, mould each piece around the chosen fillings and press carefully into patties.

3. Mix the guacamole topping ingredients together and set aside while grilling the hamburgers.

4. Mix the topping for the blue cheese burgers and refrigerate until needed.

5. For the Gruyère burger topping, roughly chop tomatoes and then finely chop in a blender or food processor. Sieve to remove the seeds and skin, combine with the remaining tomato sauce ingredients and mix well.

6. Grill the hamburgers over hot coals for 10 minutes per side.

7. Quickly grill the cut sides of the hamburger buns to heat through and place the hamburgers inside. Spoon on the appropriate toppings for each filling.

TIME: Preparation takes 30 minutes, cooking takes about 20 minutes.

MUSTARD GRILLED PORK WITH POPPY SEEDS

These pork fillets need long cooking, so make sure that your barbecue is not too hot and plan your cooking time carefully.

SERVES 4-6

4 × 175-200g/6-7oz whole pork fillets/
    tenderloin
2 tbsps black poppy seeds

Marinade
1 tbsp mild mustard
60ml/4 tbsps oil
60ml/4 tbsps unsweetened apple juice
1 clove garlic, crushed
Salt and pepper

Sweet Mustard Sauce
225 ml/8 fl oz mild mustard
60g/2oz brown sugar
60g/2 fl oz dry cider or unsweetened apple
    juice
2 tsps chopped fresh or crumbled dried
    tarragon
Pinch cayenne pepper
Salt

1. Mix the marinade ingredients together, and rub into the pork. Place the pork in a dish and refrigerate for 4 hours or overnight.

2. Using a barbecue with an adjustable rack, place the pork over the coals on the highest level. Cook for 45 minutes-1 hour, basting with the marinade and turning frequently.

3. Meanwhile mix together all the sauce ingredients.

4. Lower the shelf and baste frequently with the sauce during the last 10 minutes of cooking time.

5. During the last 5 minutes, sprinkle the pork fillets with the poppy seeds.

6. Serve the pork sliced thinly with any remaining sauce.

TIME: Preparation takes about 20 minutes plus at least 4 hours marinating. Cooking takes 45 minutes-1 hour.

COOK'S TIP: Allow the pork to come to room temperature before cooking.

INDIAN CHICKEN

Spiced yogurt makes a delicious coating for chicken pieces.

SERVES 4-6

1 × 1.4kg/3lb chicken, cut into 8 joints
420ml/¾ pint natural yogurt
2 tsps ground coriander
2 tsps paprika
1 tsp ground turmeric
Juice of 1 lime
1 tbsp honey
½ clove garlic, crushed
1 small piece ginger, peeled and grated

1. Pierce the chicken pieces all over with a fork or skewer.

2. Combine all the remaining ingredients and spread half the mixture over the chicken, rubbing it in well.

3. Place the chicken in a shallow dish or a plastic bag and cover or tie and leave for at least 4 hours or overnight in the refrigerator.

4. Using a barbecue with an adjustable rack, arrange the chicken skin side down and grill on the level furthest from the coals, for 15-20 minutes until lightly browned, turn over and cook again until lightly browned. Baste frequently with the remaining marinade.

5. Lower the rack for the last 15 minutes and cook, turning and basting frequently, until the chicken is brown and the skin is crisp.

6. Serve any remaining yogurt mixture separately as a sauce.

TIME: Preparation takes 15 minutes plus at least 4 hours marinating. Cooking takes 45-55 minutes.

PREPARATION: Allow the chicken to come to room temperature before cooking.

VARIATIONS: Cook, covered, in a 150°C/325°F/Gas Mark 4 oven for 45-60 minutes. Finish off cooking on the barbecue for 15 minutes.

BARBECUED STEAK

Skirt or flank steak is ideal for slow grilling on a barbecue. Scoring the meat before it cooks helps the seasoning flavours to penetrate the meat as well as tenderizing it.

SERVES 6

1.6kg/3½lbs skirt steak in one piece

Barbecue Sauce

60ml/4 tbsps oil
340ml/12 fl oz tomato ketchup
3 tbsps Worcestershire sauce
90ml/6 tbsps cider vinegar
60g/4 tbsps soft brown sugar
60ml/4 tbsps chopped onion
1 clove garlic, crushed (optional)
1 bay leaf
60ml/4 tbsps water
2 tsps powder mustard
Dash Tabasco
Salt and pepper

Barbecue Seasoning

5 tsps salt
½ tsp freshly ground pepper
½ tsp cayenne pepper (or paprika for a
    milder tasting mixture)

1. Combine all the ingredients for the barbecue sauce in a heavy saucepan. Reserve the salt and pepper to add later.

2. Cook over a low heat for 30 minutes, stirring frequently and adding more water if the sauce reduces too quickly.

3. Remove the bay leaf and add salt and pepper to taste before using. The sauce should be thick.

4. Score the meat across both sides with a large knife in a lattice pattern.

5. Mix together the barbecue seasoning and rub over the meat.

6. Sear the meat on both sides over hot coals. Raise the grill rack, to lower the temperature, baste with the sauce and grill the meat slowly.

7. During the last 5 minutes, lower the rack to raise the temperature and grill the meat quickly on both sides, basting with the sauce.

8. Slice the meat thinly across the grain and serve with any remaining sauce.

TIME: Preparation takes about 25 minutes and cooking takes about 45-55 minutes.

PREPARATION: Exact cooking time will depend on how you like your meat served. Rare should take 16-17 minutes, medium 20-25 minutes, and well done about 30 minutes. The times are for meat brought to room temperature before cooking.

JAVANESE PORK

The tangy sauce complements the pork beautifully. To peel the peppers, when they are cooked, place in a tea-towel for 10 minutes and peel off the skin with a knife.

SERVES 4

4 pork rib or loin chops cut 2.5cm/1-inch thick
60ml/4 tbsps dark soy sauce
Large pinch cayenne pepper
3 tbsps lime or lemon juice
1 tbsp ground coriander
2 tbsps oil
2 tbsps brown sugar
4 medium red peppers
Oil
1 bunch fresh coriander

1. Snip the fat around the edges of the chops at 1.25cm/½-inch intervals to prevent it from curling.

2. Mix the soy sauce, cayenne pepper, lemon juice, coriander and oil together in a dish.

3. Place the pork chops in the marinade and leave, covered, for 1 hour. Turn over after 30 minutes.

4. Place the chops on a grill over medium hot coals. Mix the sugar into the remaining marinade.

5. Cook the chops for 15-20 minutes on each side until tender. Baste with the marinade frequently during the last 10-15 minutes of cooking.

6. Meanwhile, wash and dry the peppers and brush with oil on all sides.

7. Place alongside pork for half of its cooking time. Turn the peppers often. They will soften and char on the outside.

8. Serve the pork chops with peppers and garnish with coriander leaves.

TIME: Preparation takes about 20 minutes and cooking takes 30-40 minutes.

COOK'S TIP: Allow the pork to come to room temperature before cooking.

VARIATIONS: Use orange or pineapple juice instead of lime or lemon.

PORK BURGERS

Pork makes a tasty alternative to the usual beef used in burgers.

SERVES 4

460g/1lb extra lean, raw minced pork
1 small onion, finely chopped
60g/2oz fresh wholemeal breadcrumbs
1 stock cube, crumbled
1 tsp chopped fresh parsley
Freshly ground sea salt and black pepper,
    to taste
1 tbsp tomato purée
1 tsp made mustard
1 egg, beaten

To serve
4 wholemeal baps
Crisp lettuce leaves and tomato and
    cucumber slices

1. In a large bowl, mix together the minced pork, onion and breadcrumbs.

2. Stir in all the remaining burger ingredients and mix together thoroughly before dividing into quarters, and forming each quarter into a hamburger shape with lightly floured hands.

3. Arrange the burgers on the lightly oiled grill of the barbecue and cook for 6-7 minutes on each side, turning the burgers, to prevent them from burning.

4. Split the baps in half, and lay a lettuce leaf on the bottom half of each bap.

5. Put the cooked burger on top of the lettuce leaf and arrange cucumber and tomato slices over it. Top with the remaining half of the bap and serve.

TIME: Preparation takes about 20 minutes, and cooking takes about 15 minutes.

COOK'S TIP: These burgers are especially suitable for teenagers' barbecue parties.

SERVING IDEA: Serve with tasty home-made pickles or relishes, and lots of salad.

FREEZING: You can freeze these burgers raw for up to 3 months, providing that the meat used in their preparation has not been frozen before.

TURKEY AND PANCETTA ROLLS

These turkey rolls look very impressive fare for a barbecue when presented sliced.

SERVES 4-6

2 × 460g/1lb turkey breasts, skinned
90g/3oz butter, softened
1 clove garlic, crushed
1 tbsp oregano leaves
Salt and pepper
16 slices pancetta or prosciutto ham
Oil

1. Cut the turkey breasts in half, lengthwise.

2. Place each piece between two sheets of dampened greaseproof paper and bat out each piece with a rolling pin or meat mallet to flatten.

3. Mix the butter, garlic, oregano and salt and pepper together.

4. Spread half of the mixture evenly over the escalopes.

5. Lay 4 slices of pancetta on top of each piece of turkey.

6. Roll up, tucking in the sides and tie with fine string in 3 places.

7. Spread the remaining butter on the outside of each roll.

8. Cook the rolls over medium hot coals for 20-30 minutes, or until tender.

9. Slice each roll into 1.25cm/½-inch rounds to serve.

TIME: Preparation takes 30 minutes and cooking takes 20-30 minutes.

SERVING IDEA: Serve with a mixed leaf salad and a rice salad.

BARBECUED RIBS

Although these ribs take a long time to cook they are well worth waiting for.

SERVES 4-6

2-3 racks pork spare ribs (about 2.3kg/5lbs)
Barbecue Sauce (see recipe for Barbecued
    Steak
or
Sweet Mustard Sauce (see recipe for
    Mustard Grilled Pork with Poppy Seeds)

1. Leave the ribs in whole racks.

2. Combine the ingredients for either sauce and pour over the meat in a roasting pan.

3. Cover with foil and bake, turning and basting frequently, for 1 hour in a preheated 160°C/325°F/Gas Mark 3 oven.

4. Uncover and bake for 30 minutes more in the oven.

5. Finish cooking on a barbecue grill over moderately hot coals for about 30 minutes, basting frequently with the sauce.

6. Cut between the bones to separate the ribs and serve with the remaining sauce.

TIME: Preparation takes 15 minutes and cooking takes 2 hours.

SERVING IDEA: Accompany with a mixed leaf salad and potato salad.

RUMAKI

Although traditionally rumaki are served as hors d'oeuvres, presented singly on small skewers or cocktail sticks, they work just as well like this.

SERVES 4

175ml/6 fl oz soy sauce
460g/1lb chicken livers, trimmed and cut
    into 5cm/2-inch pieces
8 rashers smoked streaky bacon
1 × 200g/7oz can water chestnuts, drained
1 red pepper, cut into 2.5cm/1-inch pieces
Brown sugar

1. Combine half the soy sauce and all the livers in a deep bowl. Leave to marinate in the refrigerator for 1 hour.

2. Place the bacon rashers on a wooden board and stretch them by running the back of the knife backwards and forwards along each rasher. Cut the bacon in half crosswise.

3. Drain the chicken livers and discard the soy sauce.

4. Put a piece of liver and a water chestnut on each piece of bacon and roll up.

5. Thread onto skewers, alternating with a piece of red pepper.

6. Grill on an oiled rack above hot coals for 10-15 minutes, basting with the remaining half of the soy sauce and turning frequently.

7. One minute before the end of cooking, sprinkle lightly with brown sugar and allow to glaze.

8. Garnish serving dishes with parsley if wished.

TIME: Preparation takes 15 minutes and cooking takes 10-15 minutes.

BUYING GUIDE: Chicken and turkey livers are readily available, frozen, at major supermarkets.

VEGETABLE KEBABS

These kebabs are the ideal thing for vegetarians at a barbecue.

SERVES 4

1 large aubergine
Salt
1 large green pepper
4 courgettes
12-14 cherry tomatoes, red or yellow
12-14 pickling onions
12-14 button mushrooms
60ml/4 tbsps olive oil
2 tbsps lemon juice
½ tsp salt
½ tsp freshly ground black pepper

1. Cut the aubergine in half and dice it into 2.5cm/1-inch pieces.

2. Put the aubergine pieces into a large bowl, and sprinkle liberally with salt. Stir well and allow to stand for 30 minutes to disgorge.

3. Rinse the aubergine pieces thoroughly in a colander under cold water, to remove all traces of salt. Drain, then dry on kitchen paper.

4. Cut the green pepper in half. Remove and discard the core and seeds. Cut the pepper flesh into 2.5cm/1-inch pieces with a sharp knife.

5. Slice the courgette diagonally into pieces about 2.5cm/1-inch thick.

6. Remove the tough cores from the cherry tomatoes and peel the onions. Rinse the mushrooms under cold water to remove any bits of soil, but do not peel.

7. Put all the prepared vegetables into a large bowl and pour in the remaininig ingredients. Mix well to coat evenly, cover with cling film and allow to stand for about 30 minutes, stirring the vegetables once or twice to ensure they remain evenly coated.

8. Thread the vegetables alternately onto skewers and arrange them on a grill pan.

9. Brush the kebabs with the marinade and grill for 3-4 minutes, turning frequently and basting with the marinade until they are evenly browned. Serve piping hot.

TIME: Preparation takes about 40 minutes, plus 30 minutes marinating. Cooking takes 3-4 minutes.

PREPARATION: It is important to disgorge the aubergines before cooking, as this removes the bitterness from the flavour and some of the moisture as well.

VARIATION: Use any combination of your favourite vegetables in this recipe.

MONKFISH AND PEPPER KEBABS WITH BERNAISE BUTTER SAUCE

Monkfish is excellent for kebabs as it is very firm and meaty in texture.

SERVES 4

460g/1lb monkfish, cut into 5cm/2-inch pieces
8 rashers streaky bacon, rind and bone removed
2 stems fresh lemon grass
1 green pepper, cut into 5cm/2-inch pieces
1 red pepper, cut into 5cm/2-inch pieces
12 mushroom caps
8 bay leaves
Oil

Bernaise Butter Sauce
120ml/4 fl oz dry white wine
60ml/4 tbsps tarragon vinegar
2 shallots, finely chopped
1 tbsp chopped fresh tarragon
1 tbsp chopped fresh chervil or parsley
225g/8oz butter, softened
Salt and pepper

1. Cut the bacon in half lengthwise and again in half across.

2. Peel the lemon grass and use only the core. Cut into small pieces.

3. Place a piece of fish on each strip of bacon, top with a piece of lemon grass, and roll up.

4. Thread the rolls of fish onto skewers, alternating with the peppers, mushrooms and bay leaves.

5. Brush with oil and grill for 15 minutes, turning and basting often.

6. While the fish cooks, heat the white wine, vinegar and shallots in a small saucepan until boiling.

7. Cook rapidly to reduce by half. Add the herbs and lower the heat.

8. Beat in the softened butter a bit at a time until the sauce is the thickness of hollandaise sauce.

9. Season with salt and pepper to taste and serve with the fish kebabs.

TIME: Preparation takes 30 minutes, and cooking takes about 25 minutes in all.

VARIATIONS: Try using other firm-fleshed fish such as swordfish, halibut or cod.

SATAY

Satay is a traditional Indonesian dish which is very well suited to party fare.

SERVES 4

460g/1lb chicken, skinned, boned and cut into 2.5cm/1-inch cubes

Marinade
2 tbsps soy sauce
2 tbsps oil
2 tbsps lime juice
1 tsp ground cumin
1 tsp turmeric
2 tsps ground coriander

Sauce
2 tbsps oil
1 small onion, finely chopped
1 tsp chilli powder
225g/8oz peanut butter
1 tsp brown sugar
Remaining marinade

Garnish
Lime wedges
Coriander leaves

1. Combine the marinade ingredients in a deep bowl.

2. Put in the meat and stir to coat. Leave covered in the refrigerator for 1 hour.

3. Drain and thread the meat on 4 large or 8 small skewers.

4. Grill for about 10-15 minutes, turning frequently to cook all sides and basting often.

5. Meanwhile heat the oil in a small saucepan. Add the onion and the chilli powder.

6. Cook until the onion is slightly softened. Take off the heat and set aside.

7. When the meat is nearly cooked, combine the marinade with the oil, onion and chilli powder.

8. Stir in the remaining sauce ingredients, thinning with water if necessary.

9. Brush the satay with the sauce 1 to 2 minutes before the end of cooking time.

10. Spoon over a bit more sauce and serve the rest separately.

11. Garnish each serving with lime wedges and coriander leaves.

TIME: Preparation takes 25 minutes, plus 1 hour marinating. Cooking takes 10-15 minutes.

PREPARATION: When cooking on a barbecue, if using wooden satay sticks, soak them in water for an hour or two before using to stop them from burning.

COOK'S TIP: When threading the meat onto the skewers, leave a little space between each piece so that the heat can evenly penetrate the meat.

Right: Satay and Rumaki (see page 35)

CHINESE PORK AND AUBERGINE KEBABS

Aubergine tastes wonderful when barbecued. For vegetarians omit the pork and add mushrooms and green pepper pieces.

SERVES 4

450g/1lb pork fillet/tenderloin, cut into 2.5cm/1 inch cubes

2 medium onions, cut into 2.5cm/1 inch pieces

1 large aubergine, cut in 3.75cm/1½ inch cubes

2 tbsps hoisin sauce

3 tbsps soy sauce

60ml/4 tbsps rice wine or dry sherry

1 clove garlic, finely crushed

Sesame seeds

Salt

1. Sprinkle the aubergine cubes with salt and leave in a colander to drain for 30 minutes.

2. Rinse well and pat dry. Pre-cook in 2 tbsps oil to soften slightly.

3. Thread the pork, onion and aubergine onto skewers, alternating the ingredients.

4. Mix the hoisin sauce, soy sauce, rice wine or sherry and garlic together.

5. Brush the kebabs with the mixture and place them on a lightly-oiled barbecue grill.

6. Cook for about 15-20 minutes over medium hot coals, turning and basting frequently.

7. During the last 2 minutes sprinkle all sides with sesame seeds and continue grilling to brown the seeds.

8. Pour over any remaining sauce before serving.

TIME: Preparation takes 20 minutes plus 30 minutes draining time. Cooking takes 15-20 minutes.

VARIATION: Use plum sauce instead of hoisin sauce.

Right: Chinese Pork and Aubergine Kebabs and Barbecue Ribs (see page 34)

ZANZIBAR PRAWNS

Prawns and pineapple with a fruity sweet-sour sauce make a great combination.

SERVES 4

460g/1lb king prawns, peeled and de-
veined
1 large fresh pineapple, peeled, cored and
cut into chunks
Oil

Sauce
Remaining pineapple
120ml/4 fl oz orange juice
1 tbsp vinegar
1 tbsp lime juice
1 tsp mustard powder
1 tbsp brown sugar

Garnish
Flaked coconut
Frisée lettuce

1. Thread the prawns and pineapple pieces on skewers, alternating each ingredient. Use about 4 pineapple pieces per skewer.

2. Place the remaining pineapple and the sauce ingredients into a food processor or liquidiser and purée.

3. Pour into a small pan and cook over low heat for about 10-15 minutes to reduce slightly.

4. Place the kebabs on a lightly oiled rack above the coals and cook for about 6 minutes, basting frequently with the sauce.

5. Sprinkle the cooked kebabs with coconut and serve on frisée leaves. Serve the remaining sauce separately.

TIME: Preparation takes 25 minutes plus 15-20 minutes cooking time.

COOK'S TIP: Do not overcook the prawns or they will become tough.

SCALLOP, BACON AND PRAWN KEBABS

*These kebabs are really delicious, but make sure that you do not overcook them
or they will dry out and become tough.*

SERVES 4

12 large, raw scallops
12 rashers smoked streaky bacon
12 raw king prawns, peeled and de-veined
Juice of 1 lemon
2 tbsps oil
Coarsely ground black pepper

Red Chilli Yogurt Sauce

3 slices bread, crusts removed, soaked in
    water
2 cloves garlic, finely chopped
1 red chilli, chopped
1 red pepper, grilled and skinned
3 tbsps olive oil
120ml/4 fl oz natural yogurt

1. Wrap each scallop in a rasher of bacon and thread onto skewers, alternating with the prawns.

2. Mix the lemon juice, oil and pepper and brush over the shellfish as they cook.

3. Turn frequently and cook for about 10 minutes until the bacon is lightly crisped and the scallops are just firm.

4. Meanwhile, prepare the sauce. Squeeze the bread to remove the water and place the bread in a blender.

5. Add the finely chopped garlic, the chopped red chilli and skinned red pepper and blend well.

6. With the machine running, pour in the oil through the funnel in a thin, steady stream and blend until the mixture is a smooth, shiny paste.

7. Combine with the yogurt and mix well. Serve with the kebabs.

TIME: Preparation takes 25 minutes and cooking takes 10-15 minutes.

PREPARATION: To prepare the red pepper, halve lengthwise and remove seeds and stem. Brush the skin with oil and place, skin side up under a hot grill, (or skin side down on a barbecue) until the skin is charred and well blistered. Place in a tea-towel for 10 minutes, then peel off the loosened skin with a knife.

CHICKEN TIKKA

Although this dish is traditionally cooked in a clay oven, the high heat of a barbecue is an ideal substitute.

SERVES 4

1 × 1.4kg/3lb chicken, skinned and boned

Marinade
120ml/4 fl oz natural yogurt
1 small piece ginger, grated
1 clove garlic, finely chopped
1 tsp chilli powder
½ tsp ground coriander
½ tsp ground cumin
¼ tsp turmeric
¼ tsp red food colouring (optional)
Juice of 1 lime
Salt and pepper

Half head Iceberg lettuce, shredded
4 small tomatoes, quartered
4 lemon wedges

1. Cut the chicken into 2.5cm/1-inch pieces.

2. Mix all the marinade ingredients together, pour over the chicken and stir well.

3. Cover and leave to marinate for several hours in the refrigerator.

4. Thread the chicken onto skewers, leaving a small gap between each piece of meat, and grill over very hot coals for 10-15 minutes, turning frequently. Baste with any remaining marinade.

5. Serve on a bed of shredded lettuce garnished with tomatoes and lemon wedges.

TIME: Preparation takes about 20 minutes plus at least 3-4 hours marinating. Cooking takes 10-15 minutes.

COOK'S TIP: Leaving gaps between the pieces of meat on the skewers, allows the heat of the barbecue to reach all sides of the chicken.

MEXICAN KEBABS

Kebabs are a favourite barbecue food almost everywhere. The spice mixture and sauce give these their Mexican flavour.

SERVES 4

460g/1lb pork or lamb, cut into 5cm/2-inch pieces
120g/4oz large button mushrooms, left whole
8 bay leaves
1 tsp cocoa powder
2 tsps chilli powder
¼ tsp garlic powder
½ tsp dried marjoram
Salt and pepper
90ml/6 tbsps oil
2 medium onions, quartered
140ml/¼ pint ready-made taco sauce

1. Place the meat and mushrooms in a bowl. Add the bay leaves, cocoa, chilli powder, garlic powder, marjoram and seasoning to the oil. Stir into the meat to coat all the ingredients.

2. Cover the bowl, refrigerate, and leave to marinate at least 6 hours, preferably overnight.

3. Remove the meat, mushrooms and bay leaves from the marinade. Thread onto skewers with the onions, alternating the ingredients.

4. Place over hot coals for 15-20 minutes, turning frequently until cooked, and basting with the reserved marinade.

5. Serve with the taco sauce.

TIME: Preparation takes about 15 minutes, plus at least 6 hours marinating. Cooking takes 15-20 minutes.

PREPARATION: Allow the meat to come to room temperature before cooking.

VARIATIONS: Add pieces of red or green pepper, cherry tomatoes or sliced courgette to the kebabs and cut meat into slightly smaller pieces so everything cooks in the same length of time.

GRILLED GARLIC PRAWNS

These kebabs are heavenly, for garlic and prawns make such a wonderful combination.

SERVES 4

900g/2lbs uncooked king prawns
60g/2oz melted butter

Marinade
3 cloves garlic, finely chopped
60ml/4 tbsps oil
120ml/4 fl oz lemon juice
15g/4 tbsps chopped basil
Salt
Coarsely ground black pepper

1. Shell and de-vein the prawns, leaving the shell on the ends of the tails.

2. Combine the marinade ingredients in a plastic bag. Put in the prawns and seal the bag.

3. Refrigerate for 1 hour, turning frequently. Place the bag in a bowl to catch possible drips.

4. Drain the prawns and thread onto 4 skewers.

5. Mix the marinade with the melted butter and brush the prawns with the mixture.

6. Grill for 8-10 minutes about 10-15cm/4-6 inches above the coals, brushing frequently with the marinade.

7. Pour over the remaining marinade before serving.

TIME: Preparation takes 15 minutes plus 1 hour marinating. Cooking takes 8-10 minutes.

SERVING IDEA: Serve with pickled samphire and lemon wedges.

Right: Grilled Garlic Prawns and Smoked Fish Kebabs with Horseradish Sauce (see page 58)

MINCED LAMB KEBABS WITH OLIVES AND TOMATOES

These kebabs have a very mediteranean feel about them.

SERVES 4

Kebabs
30g/1oz bulgar wheat
570g/1¼lbs minced lamb
1 clove garlic, crushed
2 tsps ground cumin
Pinch cinnamon
Salt and pepper

1 egg, beaten
16 large green olives, stoned
16 cherry tomatoes
Oil

Sauce
280ml/½ pint yogurt
2 tbsps chopped fresh mint
Salt and pepper

1. Soak the bulgar wheat in boiling water until soft. Squeeze out and spread on kitchen paper to drain and dry.

2. Mix with the remaining kebab ingredients and enough of the beaten egg to bind together. The mixture should not be too wet.

3. Form into small balls about 3.75cm/1½-inches in diameter using wetted hands.

4. Thread onto skewers alternating with the olives and tomatoes.

5. Brush with oil and grill over hot coals for about 10 minutes, turning frequently.

6. Mix the yogurt, mint, salt and pepper and serve with the kebabs.

TIME: Preparation takes 20 minutes and cooking takes 10 minutes.

VARIATION: Use ground coriander instead of cumin to flavour the lamb.

SERVING IDEA: Serve with warm pitta bread and salad so that the kebabs can be stuffed inside the bread with a little salad.

Right: Minced Lamb Kebabs with Olives and Tomatoes and Kashmiri Lamb Kebabs (see page 59)

HAM AND APRICOT KEBABS

The sweet fruity flavour of apricot is a perfect foil for the salty flavour of the ham.

SERVES 4

680g/1½lbs cooked gammon/ham cut into
    5cm/2-inch cubes
225g/8oz canned or fresh apricots, halved
    and pitted
1 green pepper, cut into 5cm/2-inch pieces

Apricot Baste
175g/6oz light brown sugar
60g/4 tbsps apricot jam, sieved
90ml/6 tbsps wine or cider vinegar
1 tsp dry mustard
3 tbsps light soy sauce
Salt and pepper

1. Thread the ham, apricots and pepper pieces onto skewers, alternating the ingredients.

2. Mix the apricot baste ingredients together and cook over gentle heat to dissolve the sugar. Brush over kebabs as they cook.

3. Turn and baste several times for about 12 minutes over hot coals.

4. If using canned apricots, reserve the juice and add to any baste that remains after the kebabs are cooked.

5. Bring this mixture to the boil to reduce slightly and serve as a sauce with the kebabs.

TIME: Preparation takes 15 minutes and cooking takes 12 minutes.

COOK'S TIP: Do not overcook these kebabs as the ham will become dry.
Baste well with the apricot mixture.

SMOKED FISH KEBABS WITH HORSERADISH SAUCE

Smoked fish makes an unusual base for kebabs. These are perfectly complemented by a creamy horseradish and dill sauce.

SERVES 4

1 smoked kipper fillet, skinned and cut into
   2.5cm/1-inch pieces
1 smoked haddock fillet, skinned and cut
   into 2.5cm/1-inch pieces
8 bay leaves
1 small red onion, quartered
Oil

Sauce
2 tbsps grated fresh or bottled horseradish
280ml/½ pint soured cream
2 tbsps fresh dill, chopped
Salt and pepper
Squeeze of lemon juice
Pinch sugar

1. Thread the fish, bay leaves and slices of onion on skewers, alternating the ingredients and types of fish.

2. Brush with oil and place on an oiled grill rack above hot coals.

3. Mix the sauce ingredients together and divide onto side plates.

4. Grill the kebabs for about 6 minutes, turning and basting frequently with oil.

5. When the onion is cooked, remove to serving dishes. Place the kebabs on lettuce leaves, if wished, for serving.

TIME: Preparation takes 15 minutes and cooking takes about 6 minutes.

COOK'S TIP: Don't squash all the ingredients up together on the skewers. Leave a little space in between each to allow the heat to circulate and cook the kebabs evenly.

KASHMIRI LAMB KEBABS

These lamb kebabs have a mild spicy flavour.

SERVES 4

680g/1½lbs lamb shoulder or leg
2 tbsps oil
1 clove garlic, crushed
1 tbsp ground cumin
1 tsp turmeric
1 tsp grated fresh root ginger
Chopped fresh coriander or parsley leaves
Salt and pepper
1 red pepper, cut into 2.5cm/1-inch pieces
1 small onion, cut into rings

1. Cut the lamb into 2.5cm/1-inch cubes. Heat the oil an cook the garlic, cumin, turmeric and ginger for 1 minute. Add the coriander, salt and pepper.

2. Allow to cool and then rub the spice mixture over the meat. Leave covered in the refrigerator for several hours.

3. Thread the meat on to skewers, alternating with the pepper slices. Cook for about 10 minutes, turning frequently.

4. During the last 5 minutes of cooking, thread the sliced onion rings around the meat and continue cooking until the onion is cooked and slightly browned and meat is cooked to taste.

TIME: Preparation takes 20 minutes plus at least 3 hours marinating.
Cooking takes about 10 minutes.

SERVING IDEA: Accompany with a yogurt and mint sauce.

BURGUNDY BEEF KEBABS

Impress your guests with these kebabs – Boeuf Bourguignonne on skewers!

SERVES 4

120g/4oz shallots or button onions,
    parboiled 3 minutes and peeled
680g/1½lbs sirloin or rump steak, cut into
    2.5cm/1-inch thick cubes

Marinade
280ml/½ pint burgundy or other dry red
    wine
3 tbsps oil
1 bay leaf
1 clove garlic, peeled
1 onion, sliced
6 black peppercorns
1 sprig fresh thyme
Pinch salt

Sauce
280ml/½ pint soured cream
2 tbsps chopped fresh mixed herbs (such as
    parsley, thyme, marjoram and chervil)
1 tbsp red wine vinegar
Pinch sugar
2 tsps Dijon mustard
Salt and pepper

1. Put all the marinade ingredients into a small saucepan, bring to the boil, then remove from the heat and allow to cool completely.

2. When cold, pour over the meat in a plastic bag. Seal the bag well, but place it in a bowl to catch any drips.

3. Marinate overnight in the refrigerator, turning the bag occasionally.

4. Thread the meat onto skewers with the onion and grill for 10 minutes or until tender, turning and basting frequently.

5. Mix the sauce ingredients together and serve with the kebabs.

TIME: Preparation takes 20 minutes plus overnight marinating. Cooking takes about 10 minutes.

VARIATION: Add a few whole button mushrooms to the kebabs.

COOK'S TIP: Allow the meat to come to room temperature before cooking.

SAUSAGE, APPLE & PEPPER KEBABS

This unusual combination of flavours makes very tasty kebabs.

SERVES 6

175g/6oz honey (set)
1 tsp chopped fresh dill
120 ml/4 fl oz white wine vinegar
460g/1lb schinkenwurst, cut into 5cm/ 2-inch pieces
2 large cooking apples, cored but not peeled
1 large red pepper, cut into 5cm/2-inch pieces

1. Mix together the honey and dill. Gradually whisk in the vinegar to blend thoroughly.

2. Cut up the sausage and place in the marinade, stirring to coat evenly. Set aside to marinate for about 2 hours.

3. Cut the apple into quarters and remove the cores. Cut in half again, crosswise or lengthwise as preferred.

4. Cut the pepper into pieces about the same size as the sausage and apple.

5. Thread the ingredients onto skewers, alternating the pepper, sausage and apple.

6. Brush with the marinade and place over hot coals. Cook for about 5-6 minutes, turning 2 or 3 times and brushing frequently with the marinade.

7. Pour over any additional marinade to serve.

TIME: Preparation will take about 15 minutes plus 2 hours marinating. Cooking takes about 5-6 minutes.

COOK'S TIP: For extra flavour, the apples may also be mixed in with the marinade. The vinegar will keep them from going brown.

PRAWNS AND CASHEWS IN PINEAPPLES WITH TARRAGON DRESSING

Add an unusual touch to your barbecue with this impressive salad. It is the perfect centrepiece for the table and it can be prepared in advance.

SERVES 4

2 small fresh pineapples
225g/8oz cooked prawns
120g/4oz roasted unsalted cashew nuts
2 sticks celery, thinly sliced
60ml/4 tbsps lemon juice

Dressing
1 egg
2 tbsps sugar
1 tbsp tarragon vinegar
120ml/¼ pint whipping cream
2 tsps chopped fresh tarragon or 1 tsp dried
   tarragon, crumbled

1. Cut the pineapples carefully in half lengthwise, leaving the green tops attached. Carefully cut out the flesh and remove the cores. Cut the flesh into bite-size pieces.

2. Combine the pineapple, prawns, cashews and celery and toss with the lemon juice. Spoon the mixture into the pineapple shells and refrigerate to chill.

3. To prepare the dressing, beat the egg and sugar together until pale in a heat-proof bowl.

4. Add the vinegar and tarragon, and place the bowl over hot water. Whip with a wire whisk until thick. Take off the heat and allow to cool, whisking occasionally.

5. When the dressing is cold, lightly whip the cream and fold into the dressing. Spoon over the salad and serve in the pineapple shells.

TIME: Preparation takes 30 minutes and cooking takes about 10 minutes.

VARIATION: For different flavours, add a little curry powder or tomato purée to the dressing, use white wine vinegar, and omit the tarragon.

PRAWNS IN MELON

Deliciously cool and refreshing for a summer barbecue, this recipe makes an unusual side dish.

SERVES 4

2 small melons
4 medium tomatoes
1 small cucumber
1 orange
Juice of ½ lemon
60ml/4 tbsps light vegetable oil
3 tbsps double cream
2 tbsps chopped fresh mint, reserve 4
   sprigs for garnish
Pinch of sugar
Salt and pepper
1 tsp chopped fresh lemon thyme, optional
225g/8oz peeled prawns
90g/3oz toasted flaked almonds

1. Cut the melons in half through the middle, remove the seeds and scoop out the flesh with a melon baller, or spoon. Leave a 5mm/¼-inch border of flesh on the inside of each shell.

2. Cut the melon flesh into 1cm/½-inch cubes, or leave in balls. Skin the tomatoes and remove the seeds. Cut the flesh in strips. Peel the cucumber, cut in half lengthways and then into 1cm/½-inch cubes. Peel and segment the orange.

3. In a large bowl, mix together the lemon juice, oil and double cream. Stir in the mint, sugar, salt and pepper and thyme, if using. Add the prawns and the fruit and vegetables, and mix thoroughly to coat evenly with the dressing.

4. Pile equal quantities of the fruit and prawn mixture into the four shells and chill well.

5. Serve garnished with the reserved mint sprigs and the almonds.

TIME: Preparation takes about 25 minutes. Allow at least 2 hours for chilling the salad, before serving.

PREPARATION: If the melon shells will not stand upright, cut a thin slice off the bottom of each one to make them more stable.

GRILLED MUSHROOMS

Use large flat mushrooms for this recipe and they will be absolutely delicious.

SERVES 4

460g/1lb large mushrooms, cleaned

Marinade
1 tbsp chopped tarragon, fresh or dried
Grated rind and juice of 1 orange
1 tbsp taragon vinegar
2 tbsps oil
Salt and pepper

1. Mix together the marinade ingredients.

2. Cut the stalks from the mushrooms and place the mushroom caps in a shallow dish.

3. Pour over the marinade and leave the mushrooms for 15-20 minutes.

4. Place the mushrooms in a hinged wire rack and cook 15-20 minutes over hot coals.

5. Brush the mushrooms frequently with the marinade and turn them once or twice.

6. Remove to a serving dish and pour over the remaining marinade to serve.

TIME: Preparation takes 10 minutes plus 15-20 minutes marinating time. Cooking takes 15-20 minutes.

VARIATION: Use large wild mushrooms such as ceps or sliced large puffballs.

PASTA AND VEGETABLES IN PARMESAN DRESSING

Use your favourite vegetables to make this salad.

SERVES 6

460g/1lb pasta spirals or other shapes
225g/8oz assorted vegetables such as:
Courgettes cut into rounds or matchsticks
Broccoli, trimmed into very small florets
Mange tout, ends trimmed
Carrots, cut into rounds or matchsticks
Celery, cut into matchsticks
Spring onions, thinly shredded or sliced
Asparagus tips
French beans, sliced
Red or yellow peppers, thinly sliced

Dressing
120ml/4 fl oz olive oil
3 tbsps lemon juice
1 tbsp sherry pepper sauce
1 tbsp chopped parsley
1 tbsp chopped basil
30g/1oz freshly grated Parmesan cheese
2 tbsps mild mustard
Salt and pepper
Pinch sugar

1. Cook the pasta in a large saucepan of boiling salted water with 1 tbsp oil for 10-12 minutes or until 'al dente'.

2. Rinse under hot water to remove the starch and leave in cold water.

3. Mix the dressing ingredients together very well.

4. Drain the pasta thoroughly and toss with the dressing.

5. Place all the vegetables into boiling salted water for 3 minutes until just tender.

6. Rinse in cold water and leave to drain.

7. Add the vegetables to the pasta and toss to coat. Refrigerate for up to 1 hour before serving.

TIME: Preparation takes 25 minutes and cooking takes about 15 minutes in all. Salad needs up to 1 hour's refrigeration before serving.

PREPARATION: When blanching the vegetables make sure that they are rinsed and drained straight away so that they stop cooking immediately.

HUNGARIAN SAUSAGE SALAD

This salad is really delicious, don't be worried about the amount of onion used as red onions are mild and sweet.

SERVES 4-6

4 small potatoes
120ml/4 fl oz oil
460g/1lb smoked sausage such as kielbasa,
    knackwurst or bratwurst
1 large red onion, thinly sliced
2 green peppers, sliced
4 tomatoes, quartered

Dressing
3 tbsps wine vinegar
1 tsp Dijon mustard
1 tsp dill seeds, lightly crushed
1 tbsp chopped parsley
1 tsp chopped fresh dill
Pinch hot paprika
Salt

1. Scrub and peel the potatoes and cook in salted water in a covered saucepan for 20 minutes or until tender.

2. Mix all the dressing ingredients together in a medium-sized bowl.

3. Dice the potatoes while still warm, coat with the dressing and leave to cool.

4. If using kielbasa or knackwurst, boil for 5 minutes. Grill the bratwurst until evenly browned on all sides.

5. Slice the cooked sausage into 1.25cm/ ½-inch slices and combine with the onion, pepper and tomatoes.

6. Carefully combine with the potatoes in the dressing, taking care not to over mix and break up the potatoes.

7. Pile into a large serving dish and allow to stand for 1 hour before serving.

TIME: Preparation takes about 20 minutes, and cooking takes 25 minutes. Salad must stand for 1 hour before serving.

VARIATION: Use scrubbed new potatoes and halve or quarter, depending on their size.

FENNEL, ORANGE AND TOMATO SALAD

This salad makes a very attractive side dish with a good fresh taste to it.

SERVES 4

2 bulbs fennel, green fronds trimmed and
    reserved
2 large, ripe tomatoes
2 oranges

Dressing
2 tbsps orange juice
1½ tbsps lemon juice
Zest of 1 orange
90ml/3 fl oz olive oil and vegetable oil
    mixed half and half
1 tsp chopped fresh oregano or basil
Pinch sugar
Salt and pepper

1. Choose fennel with a lot of feathery green tops. Cut off the tops and reserve. Cut the cores out of the bottom of the fennel bulbs and discard.

2. Bring some water to the boil in a large saucepan. Slice the fennel thinly, lengthwise, and place the slices in the boiling water. Cook until becoming translucent and slightly softened, about 3-4 minutes.

3. Carefully remove the slices to a colander and rinse under cold water. Leave to drain.

4. Place the tomatoes into the boiling water for 5-10 seconds. Put immediately into cold water. Skin and slice into 5mm/¼-inch rounds.

5. Grate or use a zester to remove the rind from 1 orange. Cut off the pith with a knife and peel the remaining orange. Slice both oranges into 5mm/¼-inch rounds.

6. Prepare the dressing by whisking all the ingredients very well and reserving the orange zest.

7. Arrange the fennel, tomato and orange slices in circles on a round serving dish. Pour over the dressing and sprinkle on the orange zest.

8. Chop the fennel fronds and sprinkle over or use whole to garnish the salad.

TIME: Preparation takes 25 minutes and cooking takes about 4 minutes.

PREPARATION: When preparing the oranges, make sure that all the white pith is removed before slicing them.

LAYERED PASTA SALAD

This is an excellent salad for a party as it can be prepared the night before. Add the dressing at the last minute if you don't want it to trickle through.

SERVES 4

120g/4oz pasta tubes or spirals

225g/8oz packet frozen peas

Crisp lettuce leaves, i.e. Webb or Cos, torn

225g/8oz cooked ham, sliced in strips

175g/6oz diced Cheddar cheese

1 red onion, thinly sliced and mixed with 4 salad radishes

Chopped parsley to garnish

Dressing

140ml/¼ pint mayonnaise

140ml/¼ pint soured cream

1 tbsp Dijon or whole grain mustard

1. Cook the pasta according to the packet instructions until 'al dente' and freshen under cold water. Leave to cool.

2. Cook the frozen peas, drain and cool.

3. In a large bowl place the torn lettuce leaves.

4. Follow with a layer of the ham, then cheese, half the onion mixture, the well drained pasta, another layer of onion mix, then lastly the peas.

5. Combine the dressing ingredients and spread over the salad. Garnish with the chopped parsley.

TIME: Preparation takes about 15 minutes and cooking takes 17-18 minutes.

VARIATION: Use your favourite hard cheese in place of the cheddar.

GRILLED FENNEL

Spoil your guests with some unusual grilled vegetables.

SERVES 4

4 small bulbs fennel
Juice and rind of 1 lemon
Salt and pepper
60ml/4 tbsps oil
1 shallot, finely chopped

1. Remove the fennel fronds and reserve them. Cut the fennel bulbs in half and remove the cores. Parboil the fennel for 5 minutes.

2. Combine the juice and rind of the lemon, salt, pepper, oil and shallot. Pour over the fennel and set aside for 15 minutes.

3. Place the fennel bulbs over hot coals and cook for 15 minutes, turning often and brushing with the lemon mixture.

4. Chop the fennel fronds finely and sprinkle over the grilled fennel. Pour over any remaining lemon juice mixture to serve.

TIME: Preparation takes about 15 minutes, cooking takes 15-20 minutes.

VARIATION: Replace the lemon with orange.

SPINACH SALAD WITH BACON, HAZELNUTS AND MUSHROOMS

Use young, tender spinach leaves for this salad.

SERVES 4

680g/1½ lbs spinach, stalks removed, washed and dried

6 rashers smoked streaky bacon, bones and rind removed

120g/4oz hazelnuts, roasted, skinned and roughly chopped

225g/8oz mushrooms, sliced

Dressing

140ml/¼ pint olive oil

3 tbsps white wine vinegar

1 tsp Dijon mustard

1 shallot, finely chopped

Salt and pepper

Pinch sugar (optional)

1. Tear the spinach leaves into bite-size pieces and put into a serving bowl.

2. Fry or grill the bacon until brown and crisp. Crumble the bacon and sprinkle over the spinach.

3. Add the hazelnuts and mushrooms to the spinach salad and toss.

4. Mix all the dressing ingredients very well and pour over the salad just before serving.

TIME: Preparation takes 20 minutes and cooking takes 2-3 minutes.

VARIATION: Add cubed avocado, coated with lemon juice, to the salad and mix in gently.

CURRIED RICE SALAD

Curry powder, coconut, and mango chutney add an exotic flavour to this rice salad.

SERVES 6

175g/6oz long grain rice
1 tbsp curry powder, hot or mild as
    preferred
4 spring onions, sliced
2 sticks celery, sliced
1 small green pepper, diced
10 black olives, halved and pitted
60g/2oz sultanas
60g/2oz toasted flaked almonds
60ml/4 tbsps flaked coconut
2 hard-boiled eggs, chopped

Dressing
140ml/¼ pint mayonnaise
1 tbsp mango chutney
Juice and grated rind of ½ lime
60ml/4 tbsps natural yogurt
Salt

Garnish
2 avocados, peeled and cut in cubes
Juice of ½ lemon or lime

1. Cook the rice in boiling salted water for about 15 minutes or until just tender.

2. During the last 3 minutes of cooking time drain away half the water and stir in the curry powder.

3. Leave to continue cooking over a gentle heat until the rice is just cooked and the water evaporated.

4. Leave covered, to stand for about 5 minutes. Toss the rice with a fork, drain away any excess water and leave to cool.

5. Combine with the remaining salad ingredients, stirring carefully so that the hard-boiled eggs do not break up.

6. Mix the dressing ingredients together thoroughly. Finely chop any large pieces of mango in the chutney.

7. Stir the dressing into the salad and toss gently to coat.

8. Arrange the rice salad in a mound on a serving dish.

9. Sprinkle the cubed avocado with the lemon juice to keep it green and place around the rice salad before serving.

TIME: Preparation takes 20 minutes, cooking takes about 15 minutes.

VARIATION: Use brown rice instead of white and increase cooking time to about 30-40 minutes.

GORGONZOLA AND BEAN SALAD WITH PINE NUTS

This salad is very colourful as well as tasty.

SERVES 4

340g/12oz French beans, ends trimmed
60g/2oz pine nuts
2 tbsps red wine vinegar
90ml/6 tbsps olive oil
½ clove garlic, crushed
Salt and pepper
120g/4oz crumbled gorgonzola or other
    blue cheese
2 heads radicchio

1. If the beans are large, cut across in half or into thirds.

2. Place in boiling salted water and cook for 4-5 minutes or until tender-crisp.

3. Rinse under cold water and leave to drain.

4. Toast the pine nuts at 180°C/350°F/Gas Mark 4, for 10 minutes. Allow to cool.

5. Mix the vinegar, oil, garlic, salt and pepper until well emulsified.

6. Toss the beans in the dressing and add the cheese and nuts.

7. Separate the leaves of radicchio, wash and dry. Arrange on salad plates and spoon the bean salad on top.

8. Alternatively, tear radicchio into bite-size pieces and toss all the ingredients together.

TIME: Preparation takes 20 minutes, cooking takes 4-5 minutes.

VARIATION: Add chopped walnuts instead of toasted pine nuts.

POTATO SALAD WITH MUSTARD-CHIVE DRESSING

Use a waxy variety of potatoes for this salad, to get the best results.

SERVES 6-8

1.4kg/3lbs potatoes, new or red variety
6 sticks celery, thinly sliced
1 red pepper, diced
3 hard-boiled eggs

Dressing
280ml/½ pint mayonnaise
280ml/½ pint natural yogurt
60ml/4 tbsps Dijon mustard and mild
    mustard mixed half and half
1 bunch chives, snipped
Salt and pepper

1. Cook the potatoes in their skins for about 20 minutes in salted water.

2. When the potatoes are tender, drain and peel while still warm.

3. Cut the potatoes into cubes and mix with the celery and red pepper.

4. Set the potato salad aside to cool while mixing the dressing.

5. Combine the mayonnaise, yogurt, mustard, half the chives, salt and pepper and mix well.

6. Toss carefully with the potato salad so that the potatoes do not break up.

7. Spoon the salad into a serving dish and slice the hard-boiled eggs into rounds, or chop roughly.

8. Arrange the hard-boiled eggs in circles on top of the potato salad or scatter over, if chopped.

9. Sprinkle over the reserved chives and refrigerate for about 1 hour before serving.

TIME: Preparation takes 25 minutes and cooking takes 20 minutes. Salad requires 1 hour refrigeration before serving.

VARIATION: Use fresh dill in place of the chives in the dressing.

WILD RICE PILAFF

Wild rice adds a nutty taste and a texture contrast to rice pilaff. It's good as a side dish or stuffing.

SERVES 4

1 tbsp oil
45g/1½ oz butter or margarine
2 sticks celery, finely chopped
2 spring onions
60g/2oz wild rice
520ml/18 fl oz chicken or vegetable stock
120g/4oz uncooked long-grain rice, rinsed
30g/4 tbsps chopped walnuts or pecans
45g/4 tbsps raisins

1. Heat the oil in a frying pan and drop in the butter.

2. When foaming, add the celery and chop the spring onions, reserving the dark green tops to use as a garnish. Add the white part of the onions to the celery and cook briefly to soften.

3. Add the wild rice and cook for 1 minute. Stir in the stock, bring to the boil, cover and cook for 20 minutes.

4. Stir in the long grain rice, walnuts and raisins. Bring back to the boil, cover and cook for a further 20 minutes, until the rice absorbs the liquid and is tender. Sprinkle with the reserved chopped spring onion tops.

TIME: Preparation takes about 25 minutes and cooking takes about 40 minutes.

SERVING IDEA: Delicious served as a side dish for barbecued chicken.

CARROT SALAD WITH CREAMY SESAME DRESSING

This salad is a delicious combination of tastes but would work equally well if chopped peanuts and peanut butter were substituted for the sesame.

SERVES 4

4 large carrots, peeled
120g/4oz raisins
120g/4oz chopped walnuts
2 tbsps sesame seeds

Dressing
2 tbsps oil
1 tbsp lemon juice
90ml/6 tbsps sesame paste (tahini)
90ml/6 tbsps warm water
2 tbsps double cream
Salt and pepper
1 tbsp sugar

1. Place the carrots in iced water for 1 hour. Dry them and grate coarsely into a bowl.

2. Add the raisins, nuts and sesame seeds.

3. Mix the dressing ingredients together, adding more cream if the dressing appears too thick.

4. If dressing separates, whisk vigorously until it comes together before adding additional cream.

5. Toss with the carrot salad and serve.

TIME: Preparation takes about 20 minutes plus 1 hour standing time.

VARIATION: If wished, toast the sesame seeds before adding to the salad.

WATERCRESS AND ORANGE SALAD

This colourful salad combination is ideal served with meat or fish.

SERVES 4-6

3 large bunches of watercress
4 oranges
90ml/6 tbsps vegetable oil
Juice and rind of 1 orange
Pinch sugar
1 tsp lemon juice
Salt and freshly ground black pepper

1. Wash the watercress and break into small sprigs, discarding any yellow leaves and thick stalks.

2. Carefully remove the peel and pith from the oranges using a sharp knife. Catch any juice that spills in a small bowl.

3. Cutting carefully, remove the fleshy segments from between the thin membrane inside the orange. Squeeze any juice from the orange membrane into the bowl with the juice from the peel.

4. Arrange the watercress with the orange segments on a serving dish.

5. Put the remaining ingredients into the bowl with the extra orange juice, and mix together well.

6. Pour the salad dressing over the oranges and watercresss just before serving, to prevent the watercress from going limp.

TIME: Preparation takes about 20 minutes.

SERVING IDEA: Serve this salad on a bed of finely grated carrot.

VARIATION: Use grapefruit instead of the oranges, and chicory instead of the watercress.

RED CABBAGE, CELERY AND CARROT SALAD

This makes a very colourful salad with a good crunchy texture.

SERVES 6-8

1 small head red cabbage
4-6 carrots, peeled
4-6 sticks celery
1 tbsp celery seeds

Dressing
120ml/4 fl oz oil
1 tbsp white wine vinegar
2 tbsps lemon juice
1 tbsp honey
2 tsps chopped parsley
Salt and pepper

1. Cut the cabbage into quarters and remove the core. Grate coarsely or slice finely.

2. Grate the carrots coarsely, and cut the celery into very fine strips.

3. Combine all the vegetables in a large bowl or in individual bowls.

4. Mix the salad dressing ingredients together very well.

5. Once the dressing is well emulsified, add the celery seeds and whisk again.

6. Pour over the salad and toss before serving.

TIME: Preparation takes about 15 minutes.

PREPARATION: Use a blender or wire whisk to mix the dressing ingredients together.

CUCUMBER SALAD

Finely chopped celery may be used in place of fennel in this recipe.

SERVES 6

1 whole cucumber
1 red apple
1 medium bulb fennel, reserve fronds
1 tbsp pine nuts

Dressing
3 tbsps corn oil or sunflower oil
2 tbsps cider vinegar
2 tbsps fresh dill or 1 tsp dried dill
1 tsp caraway seeds
1-2 tsps paprika
Salt and pepper to taste

1. Wash the cucumber but do not peel. Cut it very thinly, place the slices in a sieve and sprinkle with salt. Leave to drain for about 20 minutes. Rinse in plenty of water then pat dry on kitchen paper.

2. Wash and core the apple, slice thinly.

3. Wash and trim the fennel removing the tough outer leaves and stem. Slice finely.

4. Combine all the ingredients for the dressing and mix well.

5. Mix with the drained cucumber slices, apple and fennel.

6. Place the salad in the refrigerator or keep in a cool place for about an hour before serving.

TIME: Preparation takes 30 minutes.

SERVING IDEA: Serve decorated with finely chopped fennel fronds and 1 tbsp of pine nuts.

PREPARATION: Slice the cucumber in a food processor.

ITALIAN PASTA SALAD

This hearty salad is full of all things Italian and tastes delicious.

SERVES 4-6

460g/1lb pasta shapes

120g/4oz frozen peas

225g/8oz assorted Italian meats, cut into strips: salami, mortadella, proscuitto, coppa, bresaola

120g/4oz provolone or fontina cheese, cut into strips

15 black olives, halved and pitted

60ml/4 tbsps small capers

1 small red onion or 2 shallots, chopped

175g/6oz oyster mushrooms, trimmed and sliced

Dressing

3 tbsps white wine vinegar

120ml/4 fl oz olive oil

½ clove garlic, crushed

1 tsp fennel seeds, crushed

1 tbsp chopped parsley

1 tbsp chopped basil

1 tbsp mustard

Salt and pepper

1. Cook the pasta in a large saucepan of boiling water with a pinch of salt and 1 tbsp oil. Cook for about 10 minutes or until 'al dente'.

2. Add the frozen peas during the last 3 minutes of cooking time.

3. Drain the pasta and peas and rinse under hot water. Leave in cold water until ready to use.

4. Mix the pasta and peas with the Italian meats and cheeses, olives, capers, chopped onion or shallot and sliced mushrooms.

5. Mix together the dressing ingredients, pour over the salad and toss all the ingredients together to coat. Do not over-mix.

6. Leave the salad to chill for up to 1 hour before serving.

TIME: Preparation takes about 20 minutes and cooking takes 10-12 minutes. The salad must chill for 1 hour before serving.

VARIATION: If wished, use mange tout peas, diagonally sliced, and cook for 1-2 minutes.

CAESAR SALAD

This is a famous American salad and is very tasty for something that was supposedly made up from the only ingredients left in the kitchen!

SERVES 4-6

1 large or 2 small heads cos lettuce
8 slices white bread, crusts removed
120ml/4 fl oz oil
1 clove garlic, peeled
1 small can anchovies
90g/3oz fresh Parmesan cheese

Dressing
1 egg
120ml/4 fl oz olive oil
Juice of 1 lemon
1 clove garlic, crushed
Salt and pepper

1. Wash the lettuce and dry well. Tear into bite-size pieces and place in a large salad bowl, or four individual bowls.

2. Cut the slices of bread into 1.25cm/½-inch dice.

3. Heat the vegetable oil in a small frying pan.

4. Add the garlic and cubes of bread. Lower the heat slightly and keep stirring the cubes of bread to brown them evenly.

5. When they are golden brown and crisp, remove them to kitchen paper to drain.

6. Add the anchovies to the lettuce and sprinkle on the fried croûtons.

7. To prepare the dressing, place the egg in boiling water for 1 minute. Break into a small bowl and combine with the remaining dressing ingredients, whisking very well.

8. Pour the dressing over the salad and toss.

9. Using a cheese slicer, shave off thin slices of Parmesan cheese and add to the salad.

TIME: Preparation takes about 20 minutes, plus 3 minutes cooking time.

VARIATION: Grate the Parmesan and add it to the salad with the dressing.

GREEK SALAD

This salad is a lively combination of tastes and is the classic salad served in all Greek restaurants.

SERVES 4

1 head cos lettuce
16 black olives, pitted
120g/4oz crumbled feta cheese
1 small can anchovies, drained
8 mild pickled peppers
60g/2oz cherry tomatoes, halved
½ cucumber, cut in small dice
2 tbsps chopped fresh oregano or 1 tbsp
    dried oregano

Dressing
120ml/4 fl oz olive oil
3 tbsps red wine vinegar
1 clove garlic, crushed
Salt and pepper

1. Wash and dry the cos lettuce and tear the leaves into bite-size pieces.

2. Place the leaves in a large salad bowl and arrange or scatter all the other ingredients on top of the lettuce.

3. If the anchovies are large, cut them into thinner strips or chop into small pieces.

4. Sprinkle the fresh or dried oregano over all the ingredients in the salad bowl.

5. Mix the dressing together well and pour over the salad just before serving.

TIME: Preparation takes 15 minutes.

VARIATION: Use virgin olive oil in the dressing for even more flavour.

FRUIT KEBABS

These unusual kebabs make the ideal dessert for a barbecue.

SERVES 4

4 peaches or apricots, halved
Small punnet strawberries
3-4 kiwi fruit, sliced
3-4 slices fresh pineapple, segmented
Mint leaves (optional)
Lemon juice
Honey

1. Thread alternate pieces of fruit onto skewers, interspersed with some fresh mint leaves.

2. Sprinkle with a little lemon juice and brush with some honey.

3. Barbecue for about 8 minutes.

TIME: Preparation takes about 15 minutes and cooking takes 8 minutes.

VARIATION: Use other fruit such as apples, mango, figs, bananas, paw paw, or nectarines.

SERVING IDEA: Serve with whipped cream or greek yogurt.

SUMMER PUDDING

This dessert must be prepared at least 24 hours before it is needed and is an excellent way of using up a glut of soft summer fruits. Most soft fruits can be used, but raspberries and redcurrants should predominate, both for taste and final colour.

SERVES 6

900g/2lbs mixed soft fruit (i.e. raspberries, redcurrants, blackcurrants, strawberries)
8 slices day-old white bread with crusts removed
120g/4oz caster sugar (more or less can be used according to taste)

1. Prepare and wash the fruit and place in a heavy-based saucepan together with the caster sugar. Cook over a low heat for 5-10 minutes until the sugar dissolves and the juices start to run.

2. Line the base and sides of a greased 1 litre/1¾ pint pudding basin with some of the slices of bread, trimming the slices so they fit tightly.

3. Pack in the fruit and enough juice to stain the bread. Cover with the remaining slices, pour on a little more juice and retain the rest.

4. Cover the basin with a saucer or plate which rests on the pudding itself. Add a 460g/1lb weight or heavy tin or jar, in order to compress the pudding. Leave to stand overnight in the refrigerator.

5. To turn out, loosen the sides with a palette knife and invert onto a serving plate.

TIME: Preparation takes about 20 minutes plus about 10 minutes cooking time. The pudding must be refrigerated for at least 24 hours before being served.

COOK'S TIP: Use the reserved juices to baste the unmoulded pudding to cover any white patches.

SERVING IDEA: Serve with double or clotted cream, and any remaining juice.

EASY RASPBERRY MOUSSE

Keep the children happy with this delicious, but simple dessert which can be prepared in advance.

SERVES 4

175g/6oz evaporated milk
375g/13oz can of raspberries
1 packet raspberry jelly
1 egg white

---

1. Chill the evaporated milk for at least an hour in the refrigerator.

2. Drain the liquid from the can of raspberries into a measuring jug and make up to 280ml/½ pint with water. Use this liquid to make the jelly, following the packet instructions. Leave to cool until just on setting point.

3. Whisk the egg white until stiff. Whisk the evaporated milk until thick and frothy. Whisk the jelly and add the evaporated milk. Continue whisking for a couple more minutes.

4. Fold in the beaten egg white and the raspberries. Turn into a mould and leave to set.

TIME: Preparation takes about 3 hours, including chilling.

SERVING IDEA: Turn out the mousse onto a serving plate and decorate with whipped cream and raspberries. Keep in the fridge until serving time.

VANILLA FLOATING ISLANDS

A delightful dessert to serve after a barbecue.

SERVES 6

Custard
430ml/¾ pint milk
4 egg yolks
60g/2oz caster sugar
1 level tbsp cornflour
Few drops vanilla essence

Meringue Islands
4 egg whites
150g/5oz caster sugar
2 tbsps crushed praline

1. Heat the milk in a saucepan until almost boiling. In a mixing bowl, mix together the egg yolks, sugar and cornflour. Slowly add the hot milk and stir well.

2. Strain the mixture back into the saucepan and set over a low heat. Stir until the custard thickens but do not allow the mixture to boil. Turn the custard into a clean bowl and add a few drops of vanilla essence. Stir the mixture, to prevent a skin forming, until it is cold. Cover with cling film.

3. In a medium-sized mixing bowl, whisk the egg whites until stiff. Add the sugar, a spoonful at a time, beating well after each addition.

4. Fill a frying pan with water and bring to simmering point. With a tablespoon, scoop out mounds of meringue mixture and drop gently into the water, using another tablespoon to help remove the mixture from the first spoon. Only cook four or five at a time.

5. Poach the meringues gently for 3 or 4 minutes, then scoop from the water with a draining spoon and place on kitchen paper to drain. Continue poaching all the meringue mixture in the same way.

6. Place the custard in a large serving dish and gently pile the poached meringues on top. Chill until ready to serve then sprinkle with crushed praline.

TIME: Preparation takes about 45 minutes.

VARIATIONS: **Chocolate Floating Islands** For the custard, continue as before, but flavour the custard with one tablespoon of cocoa powder dissolved in a little hot water until it makes a smooth paste. Omit the vanilla essence. Add the chocolate mixture to the custard, beating well. When the dish is assembled, sprinkle with cocoa powder until the dish is finely covered.
Coffee Floating Islands For the custard, continue as before, but flavour the custard with a level tablespoon of coffee granules mixed to a smooth paste with a little hot water. Add this to the custard, to taste, beating well. Omit the vanilla essence. When the dish is assembled, sprinkle with finely grated nutmeg until the dish is finely covered.

Index